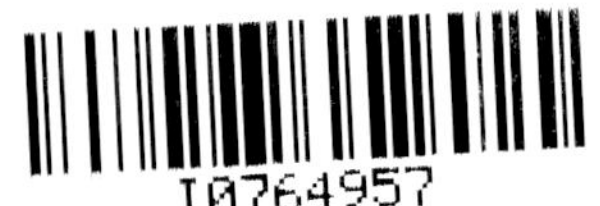

DINOSAUR

COLORING BOOK FOR KIDS

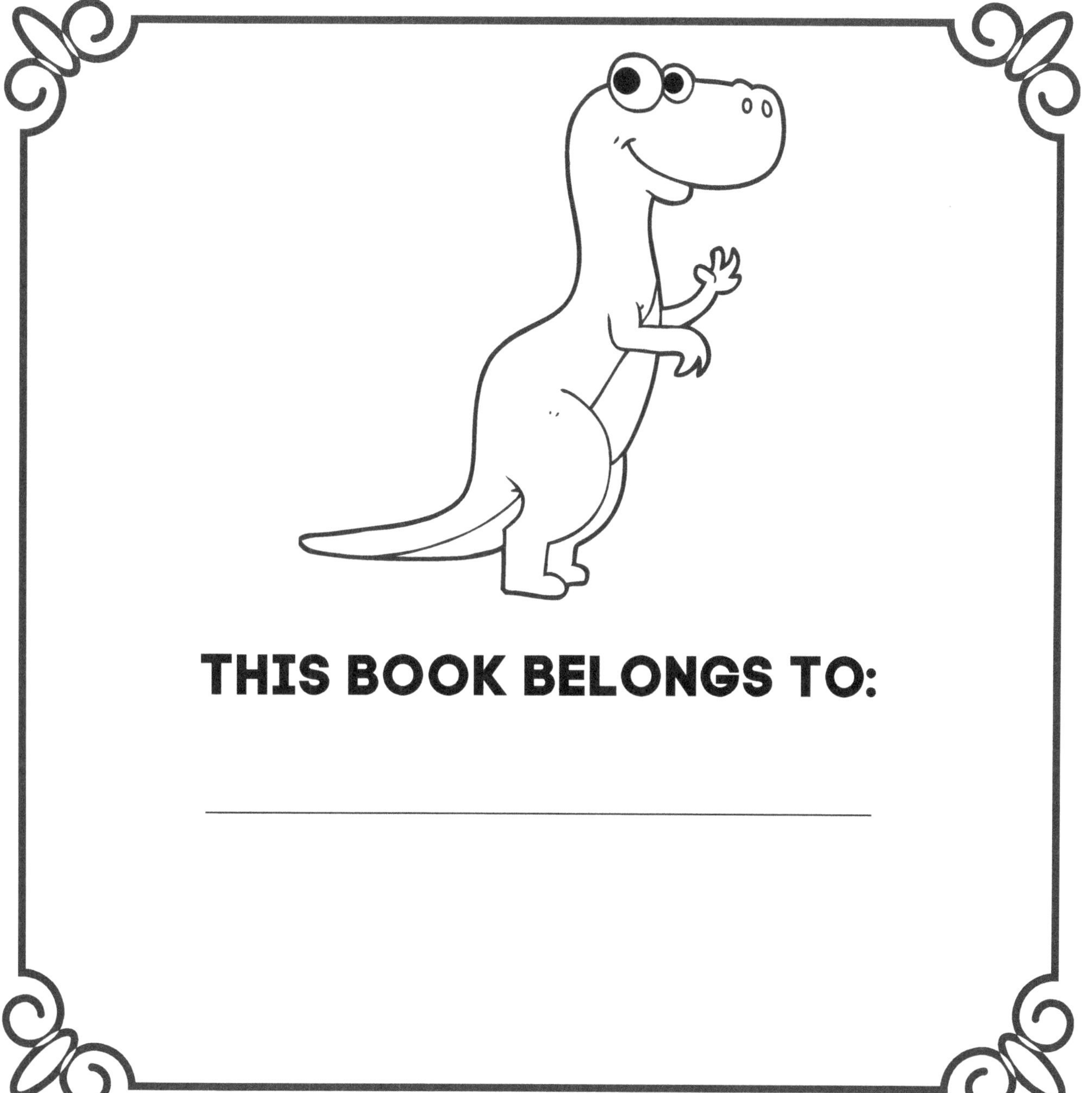

THIS BOOK BELONGS TO:

____

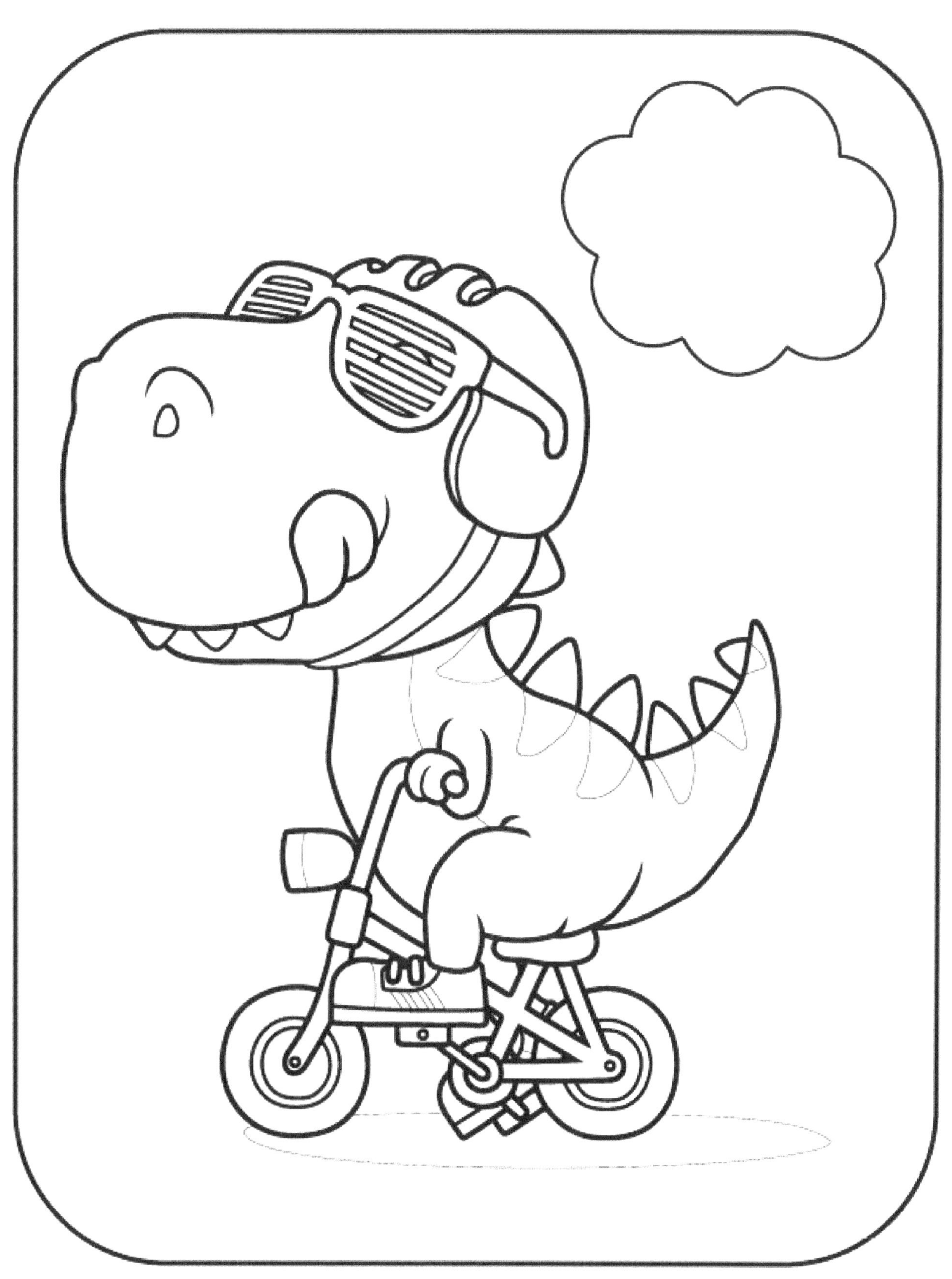

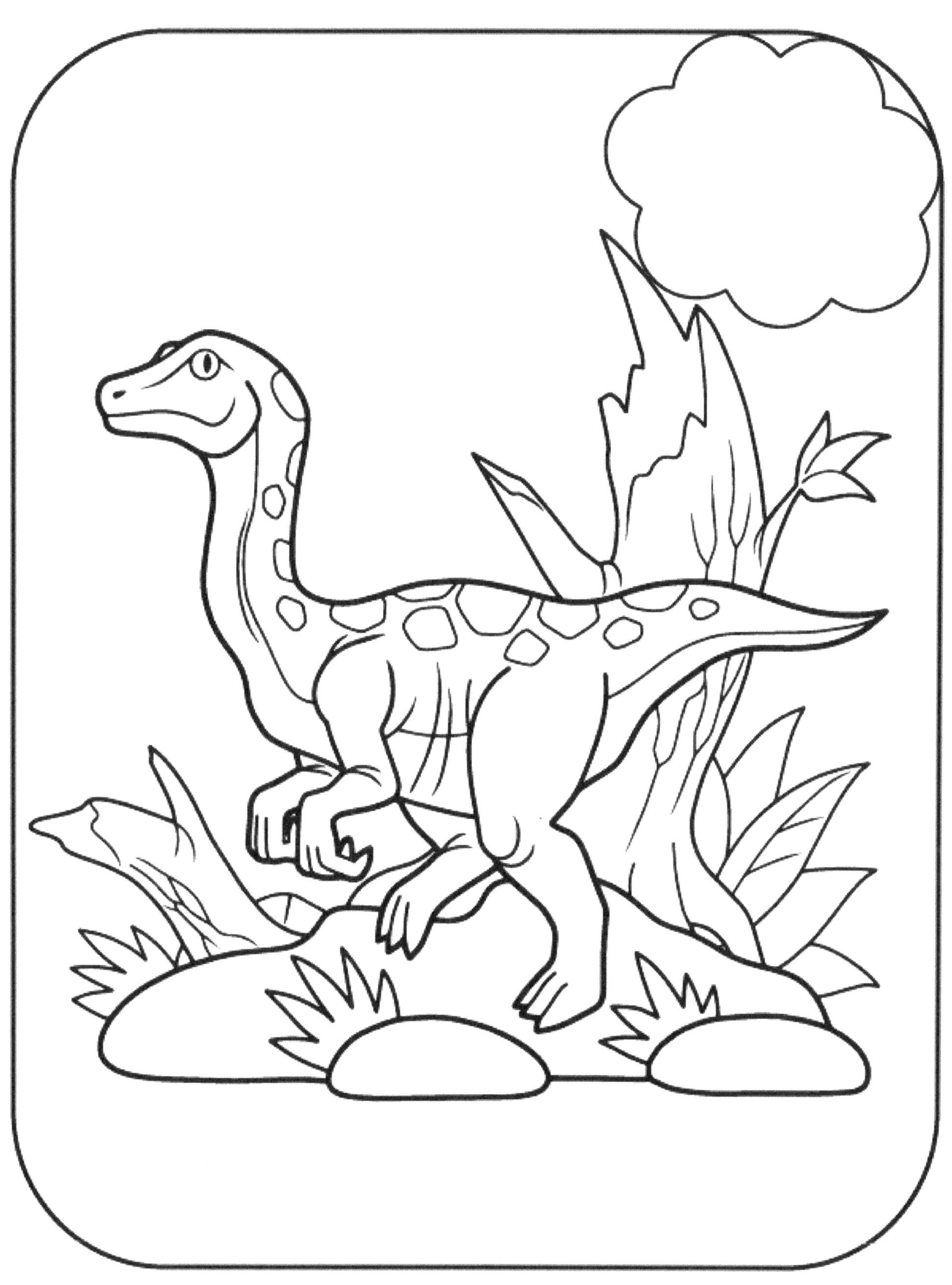

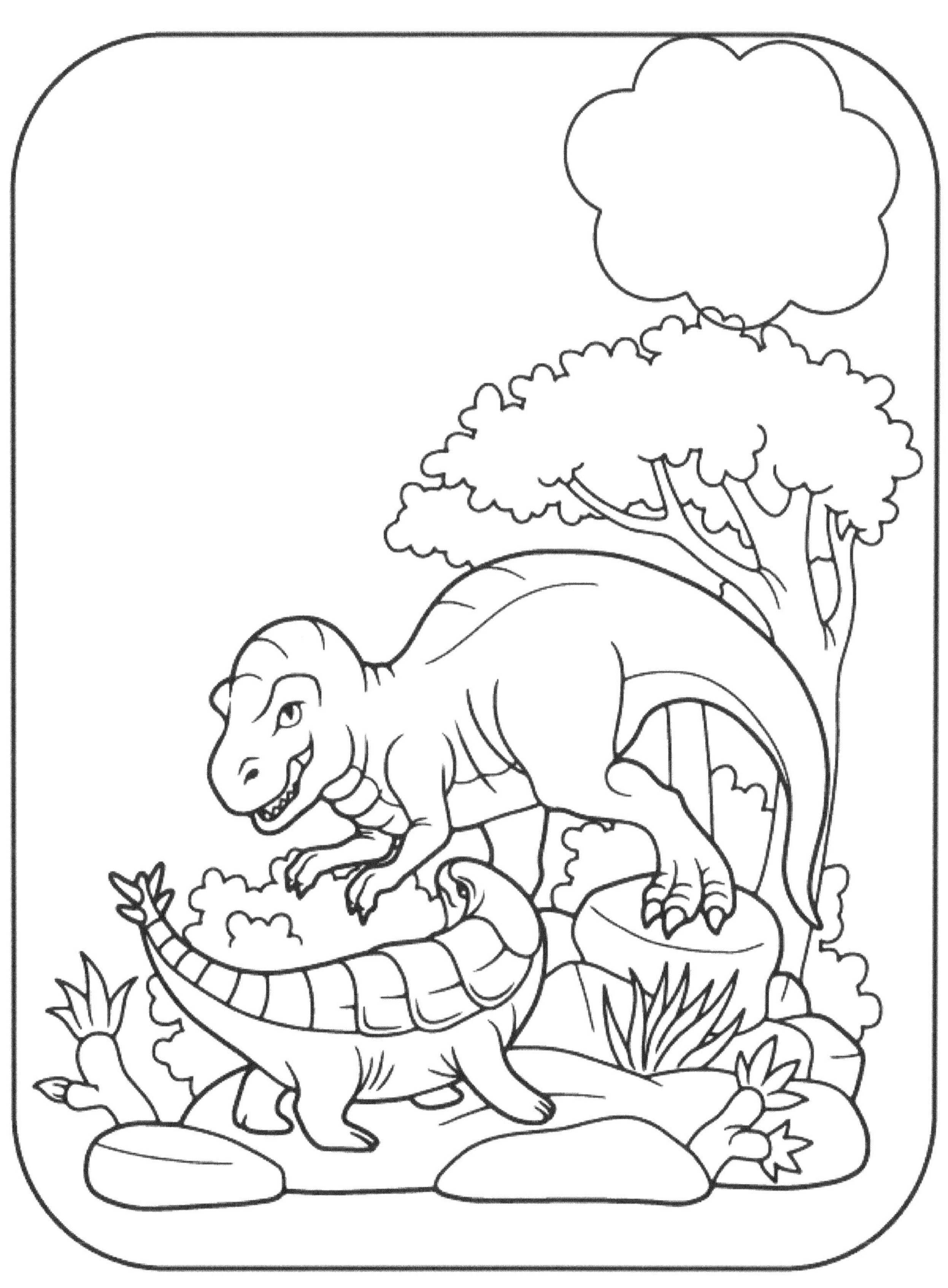

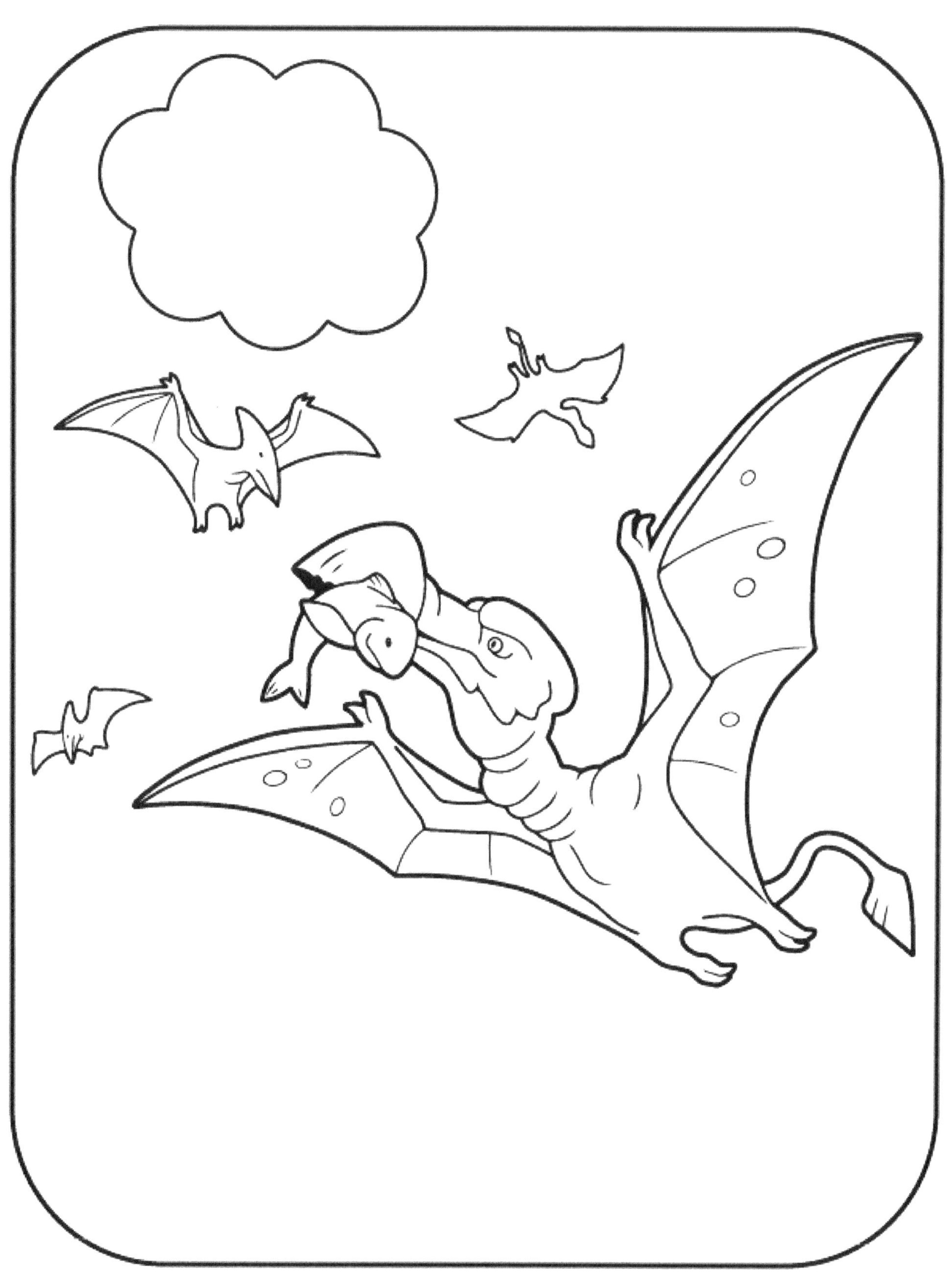

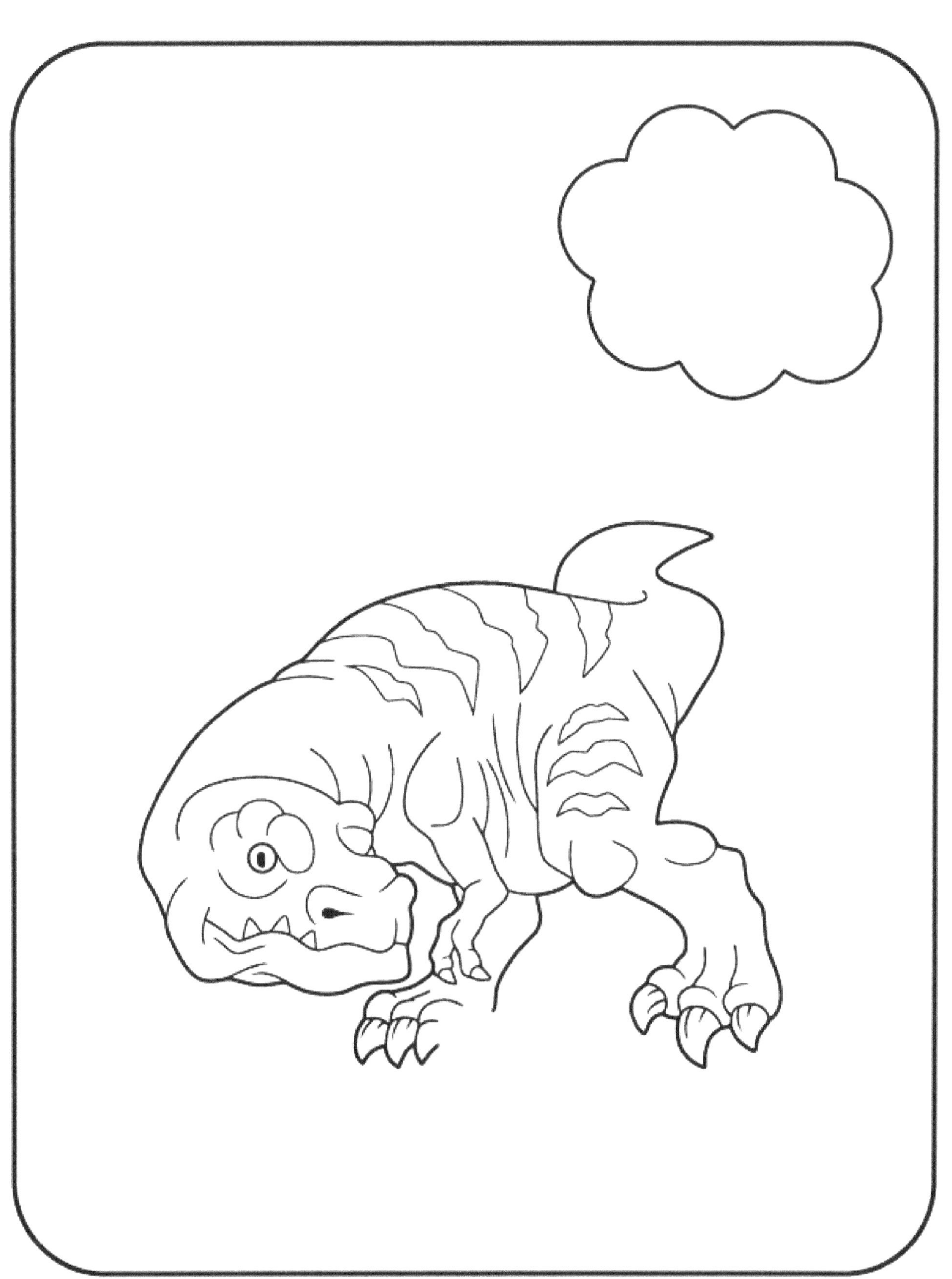

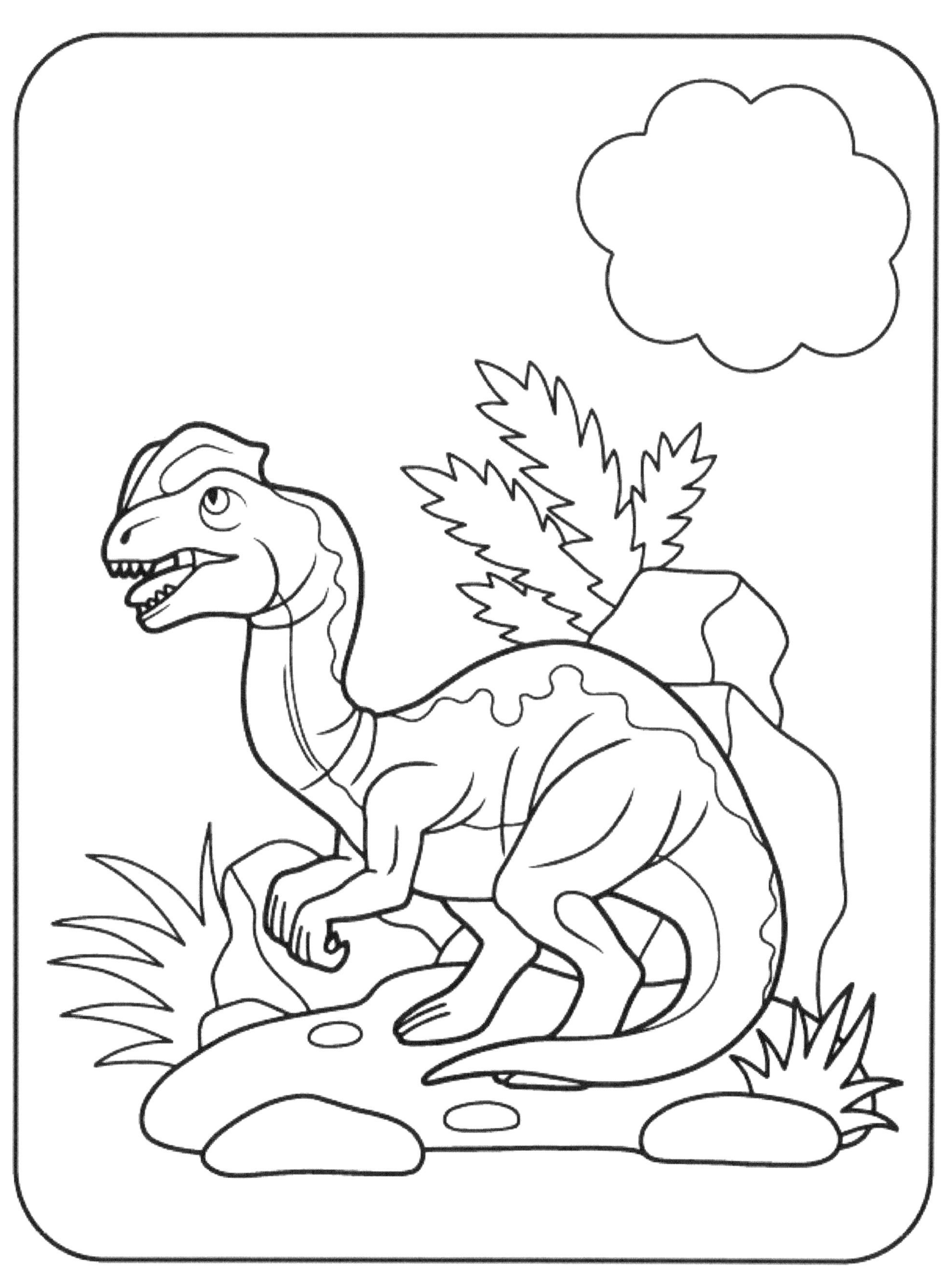

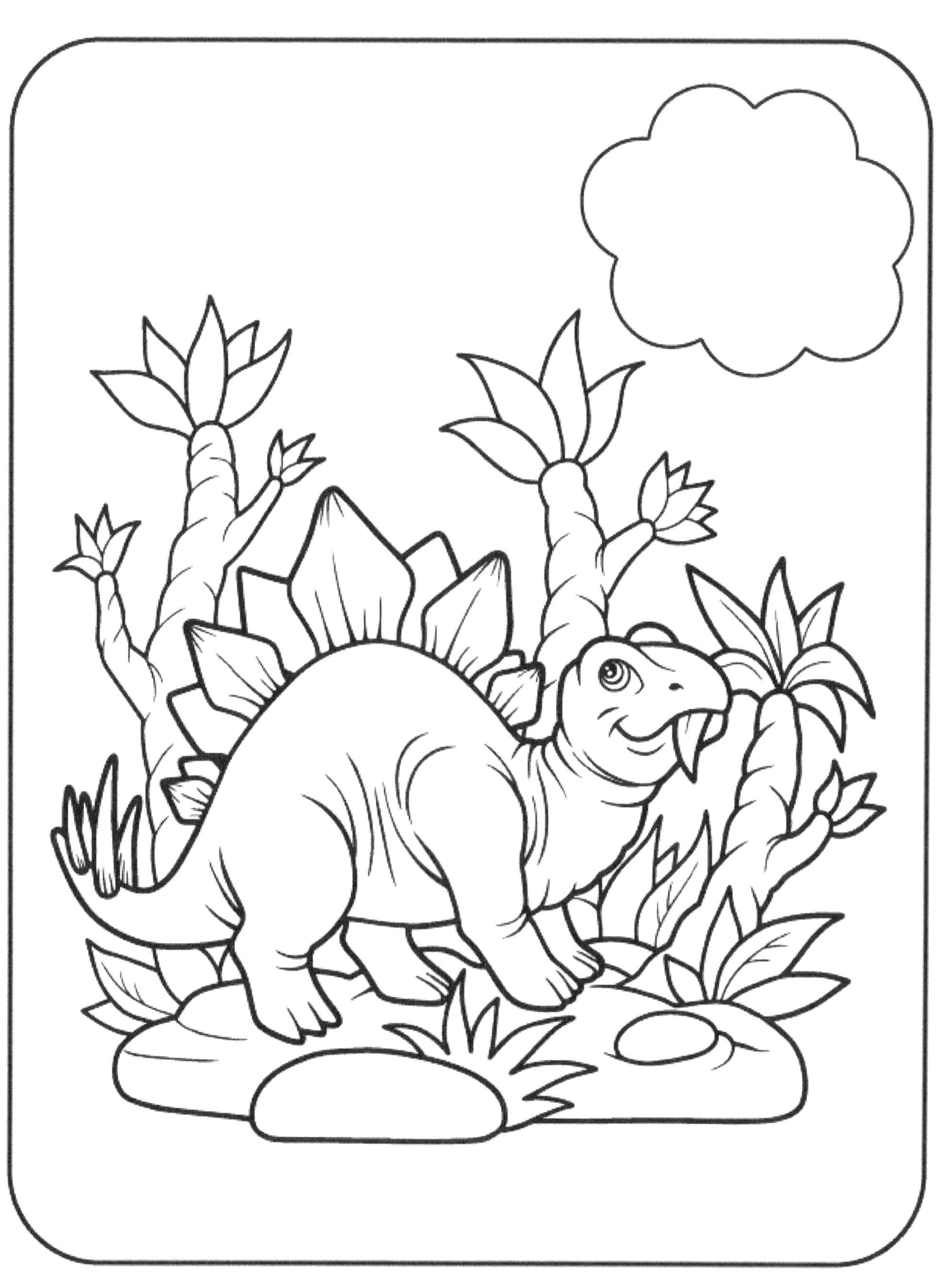

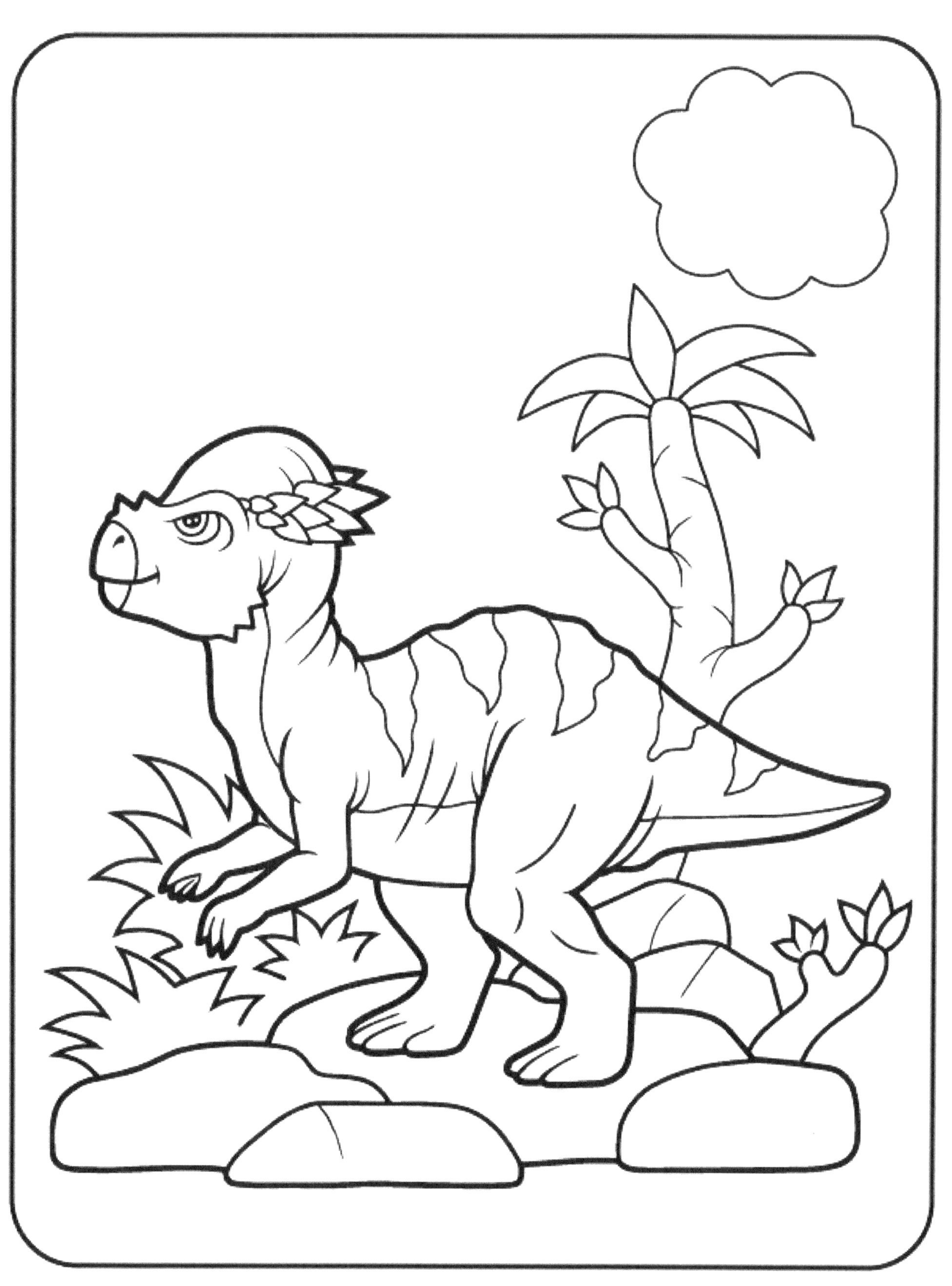

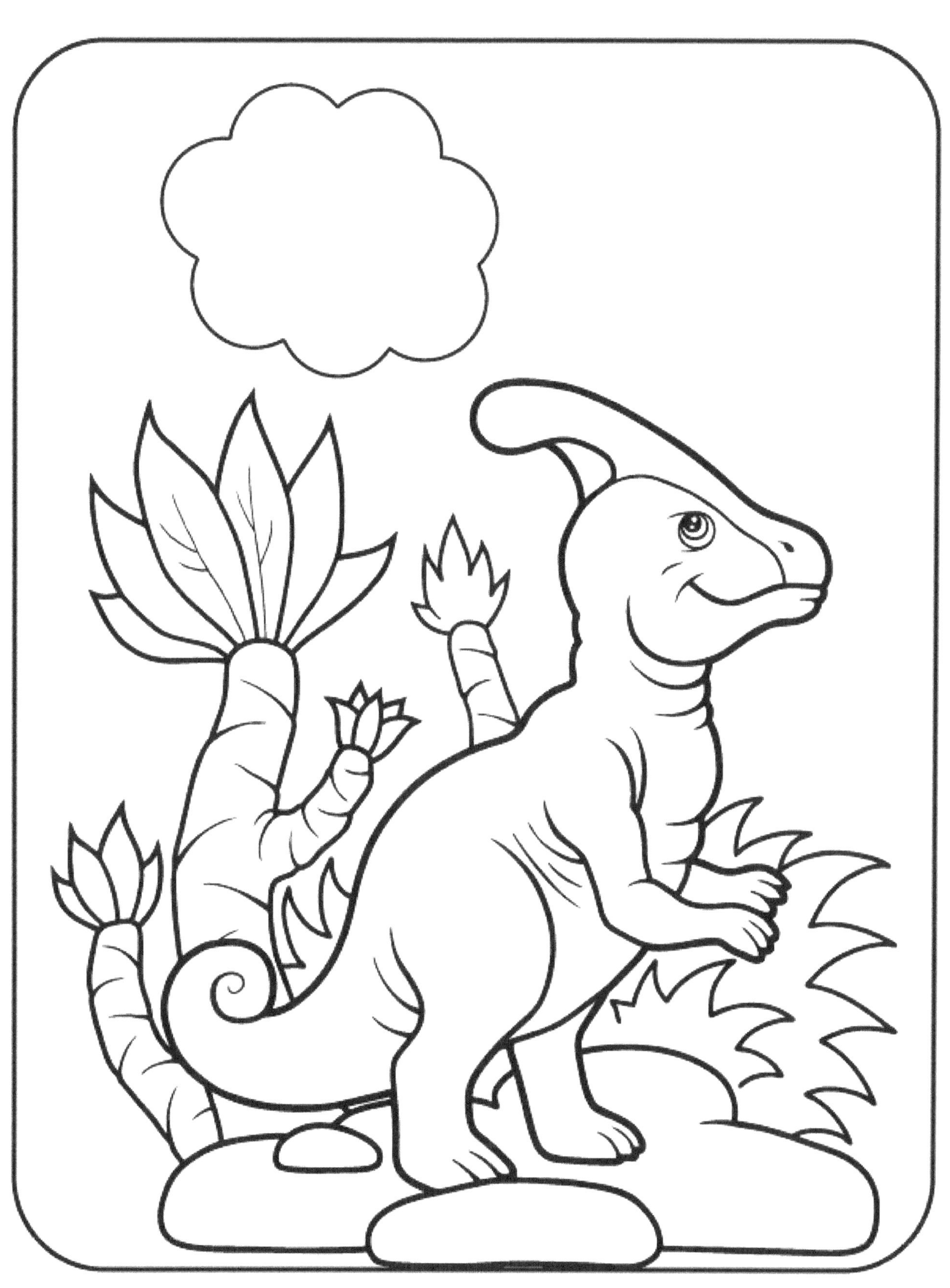

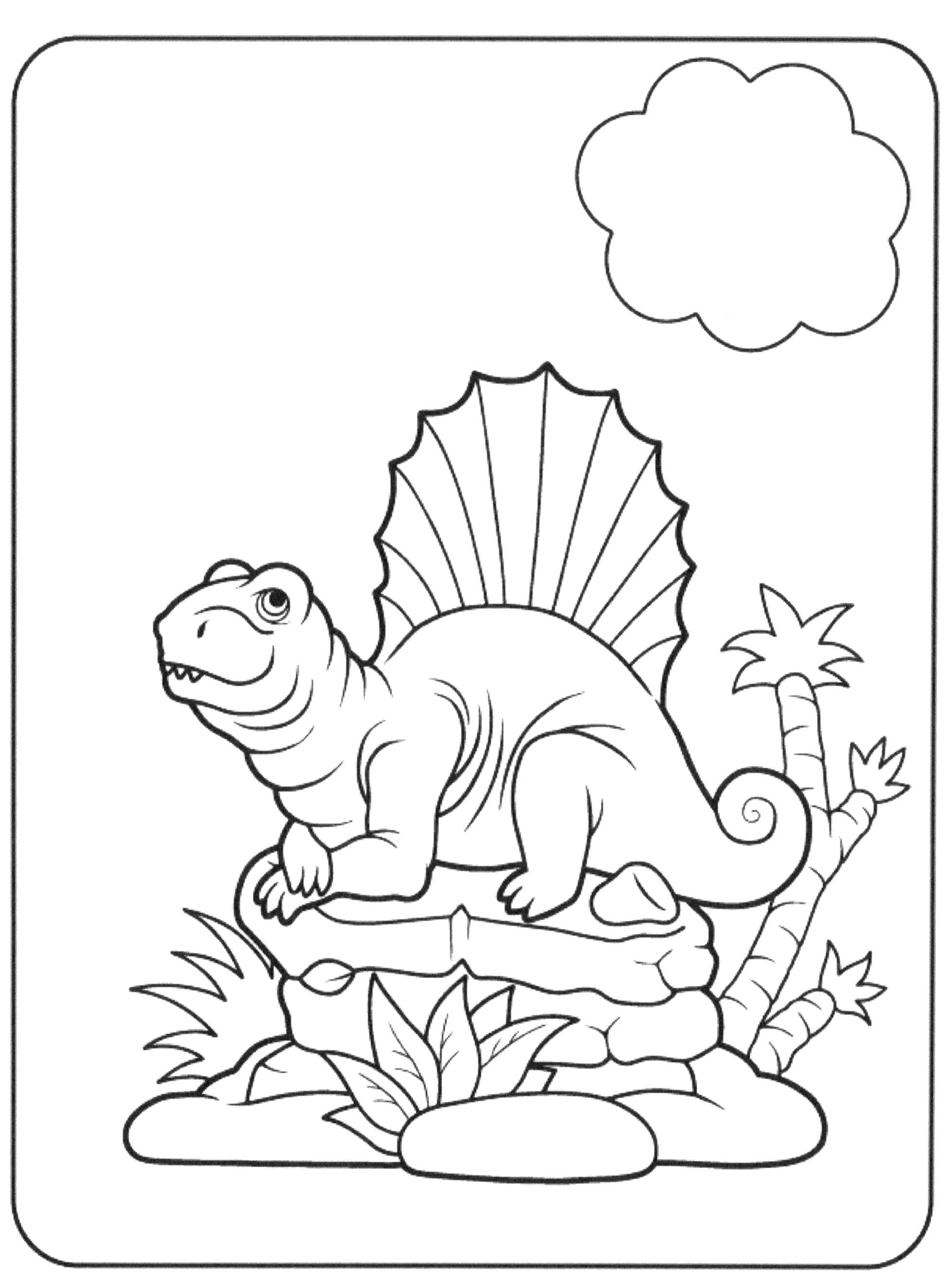

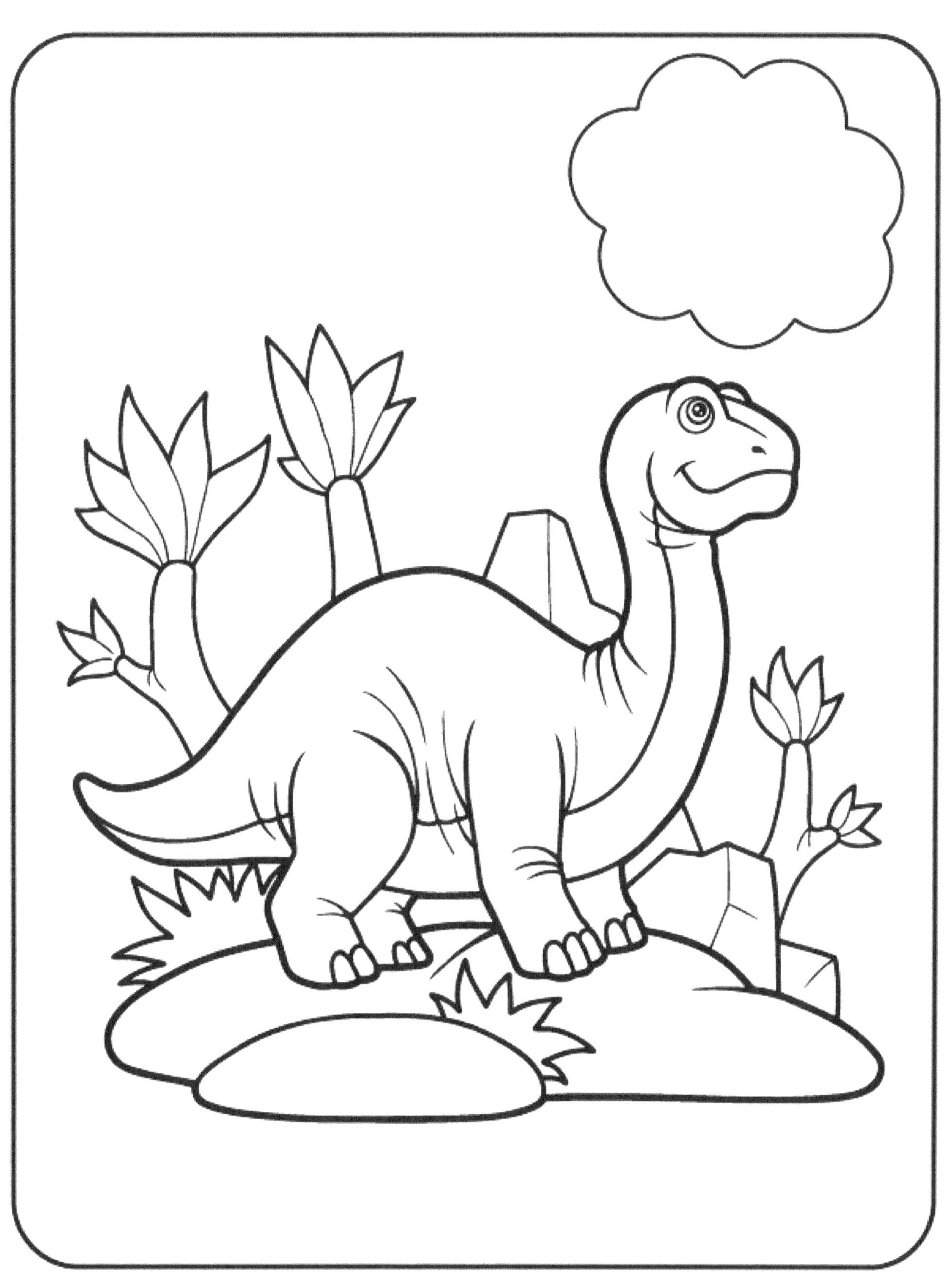

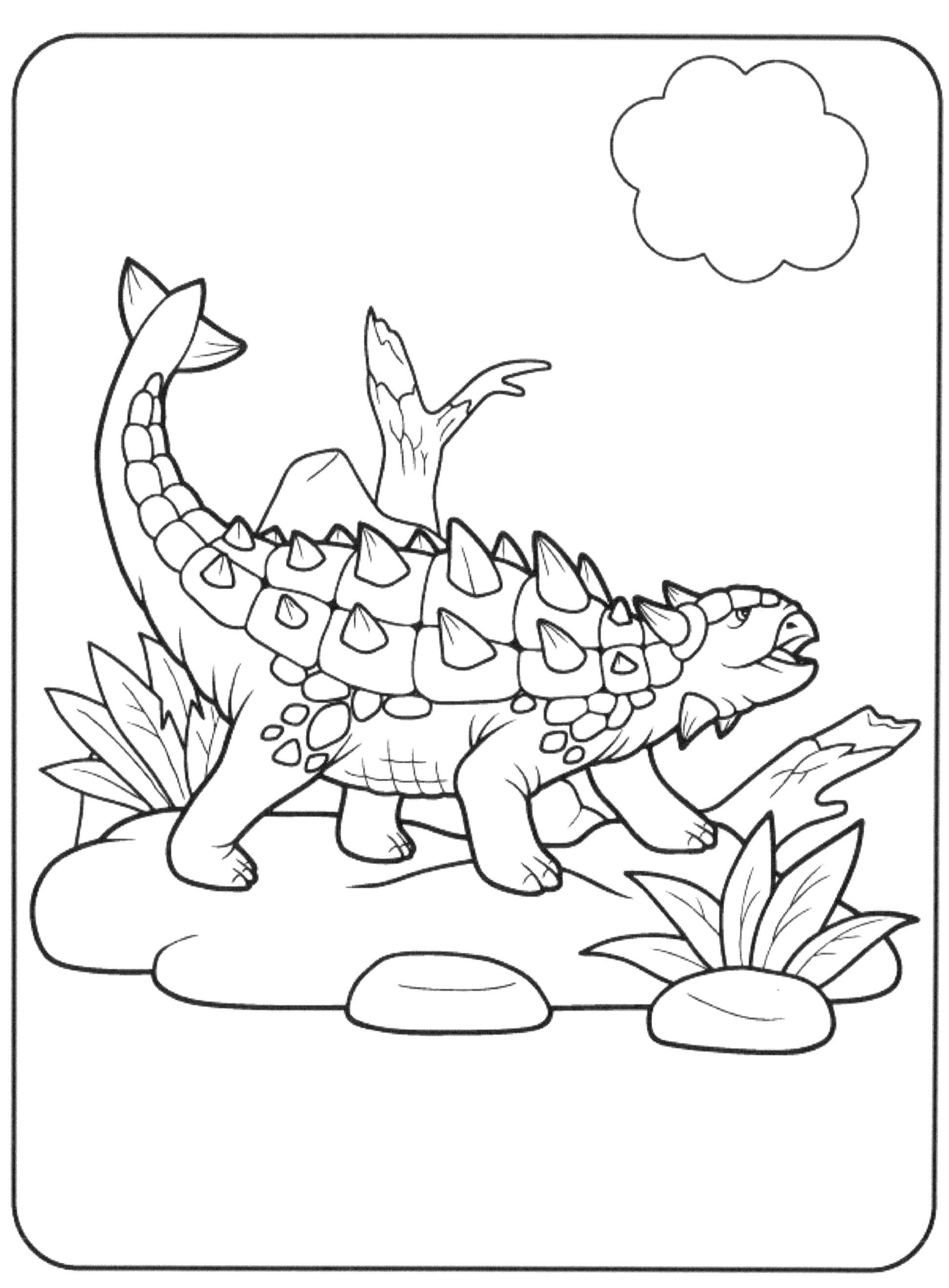

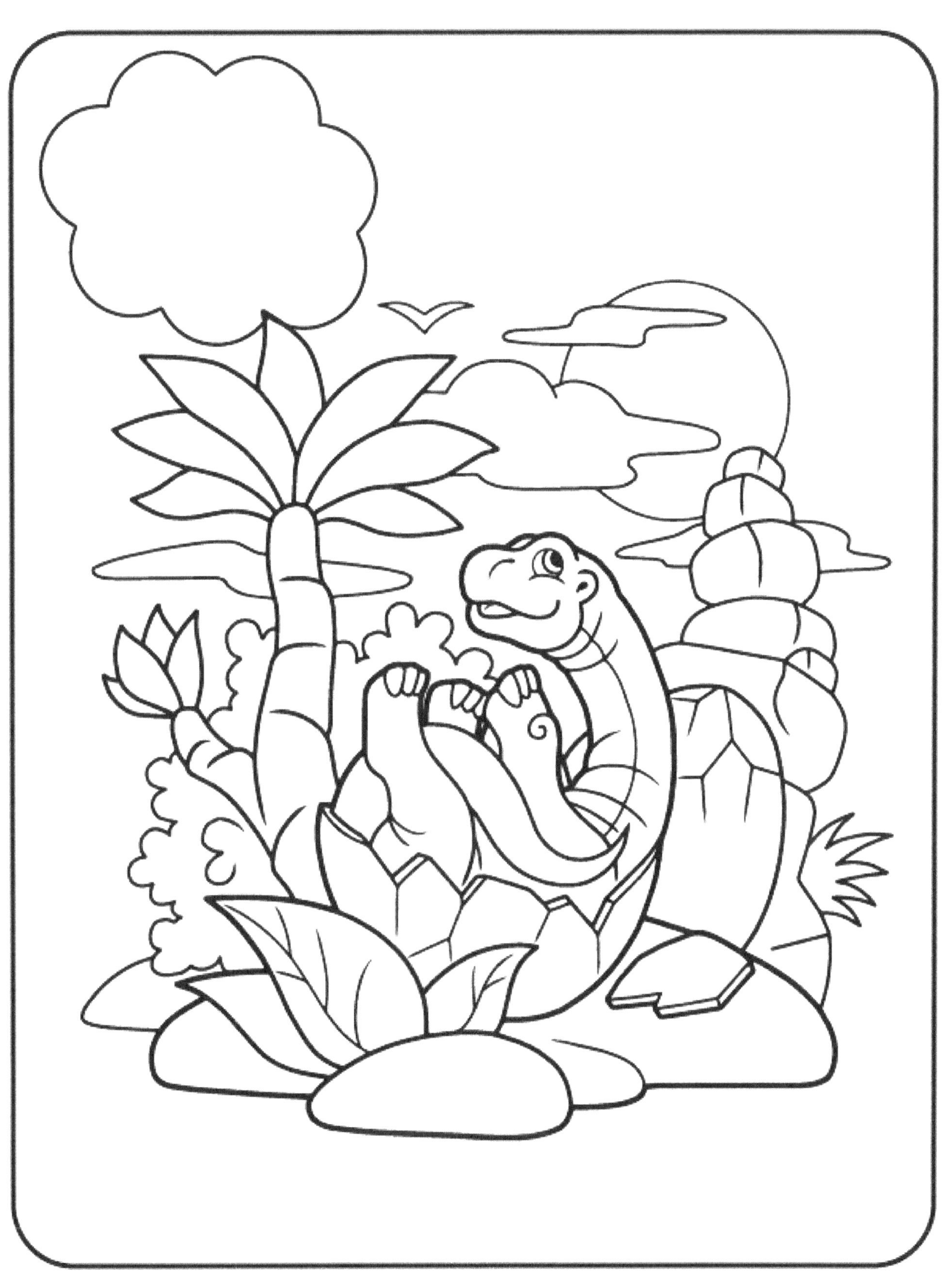

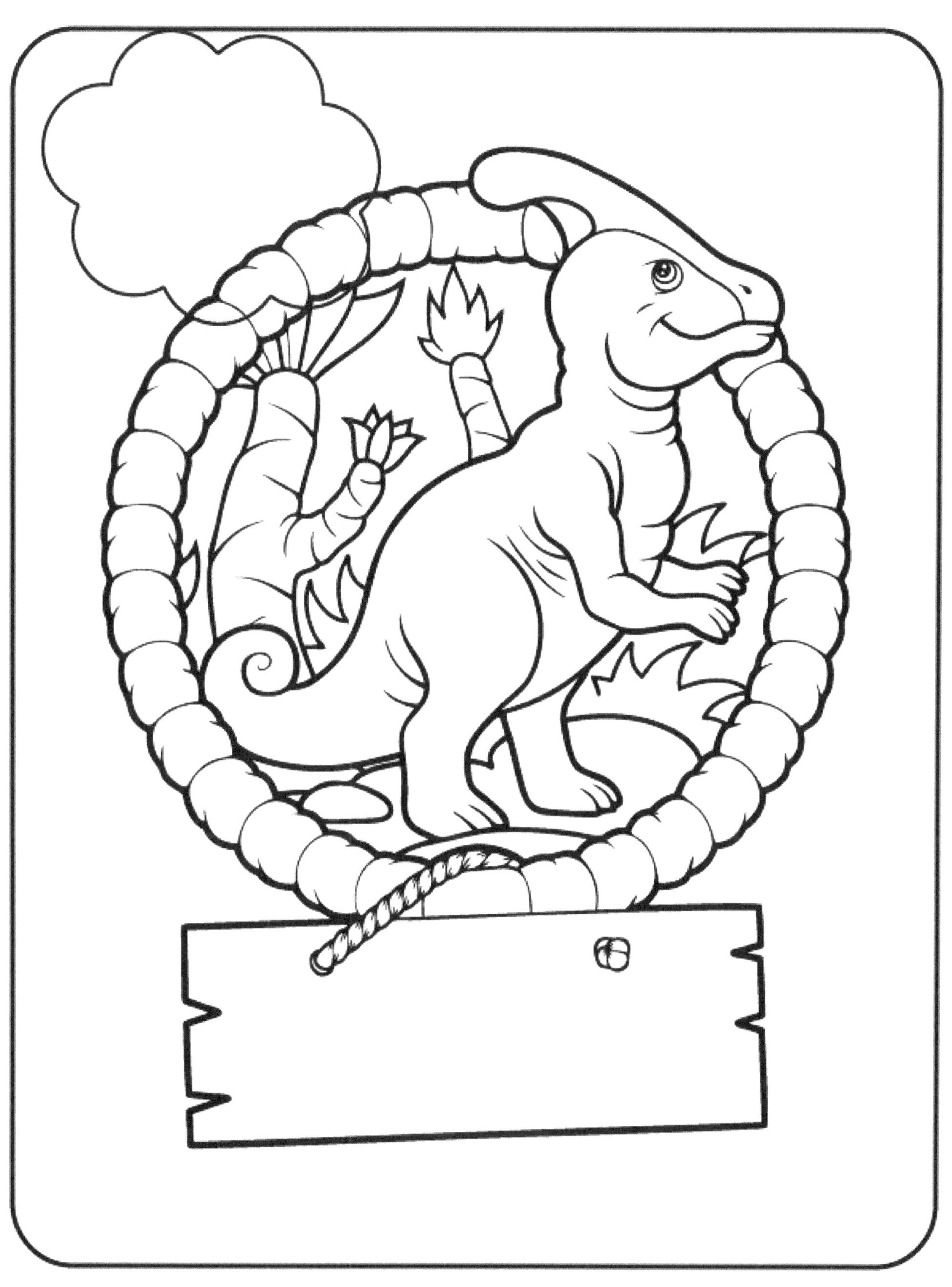

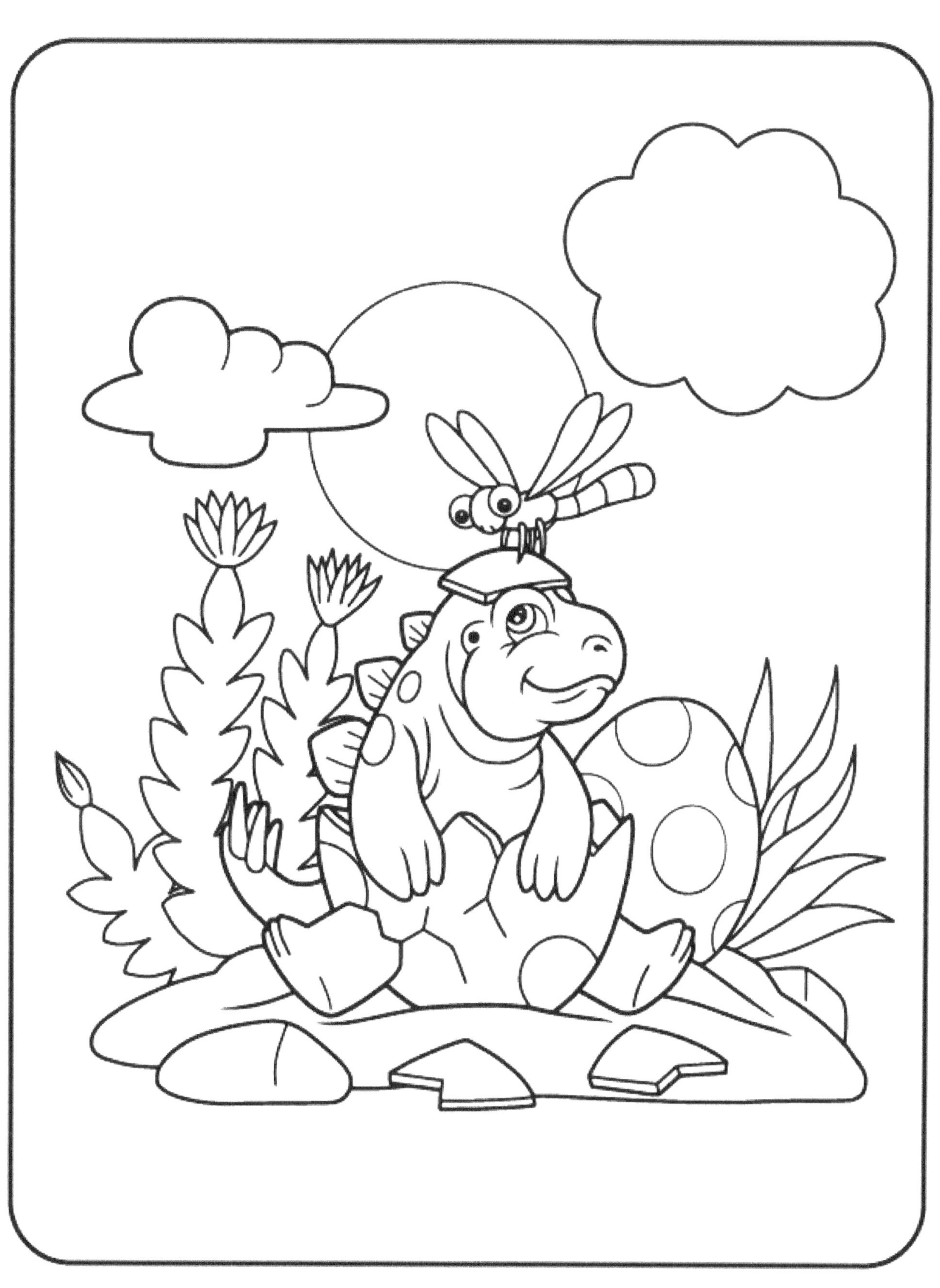

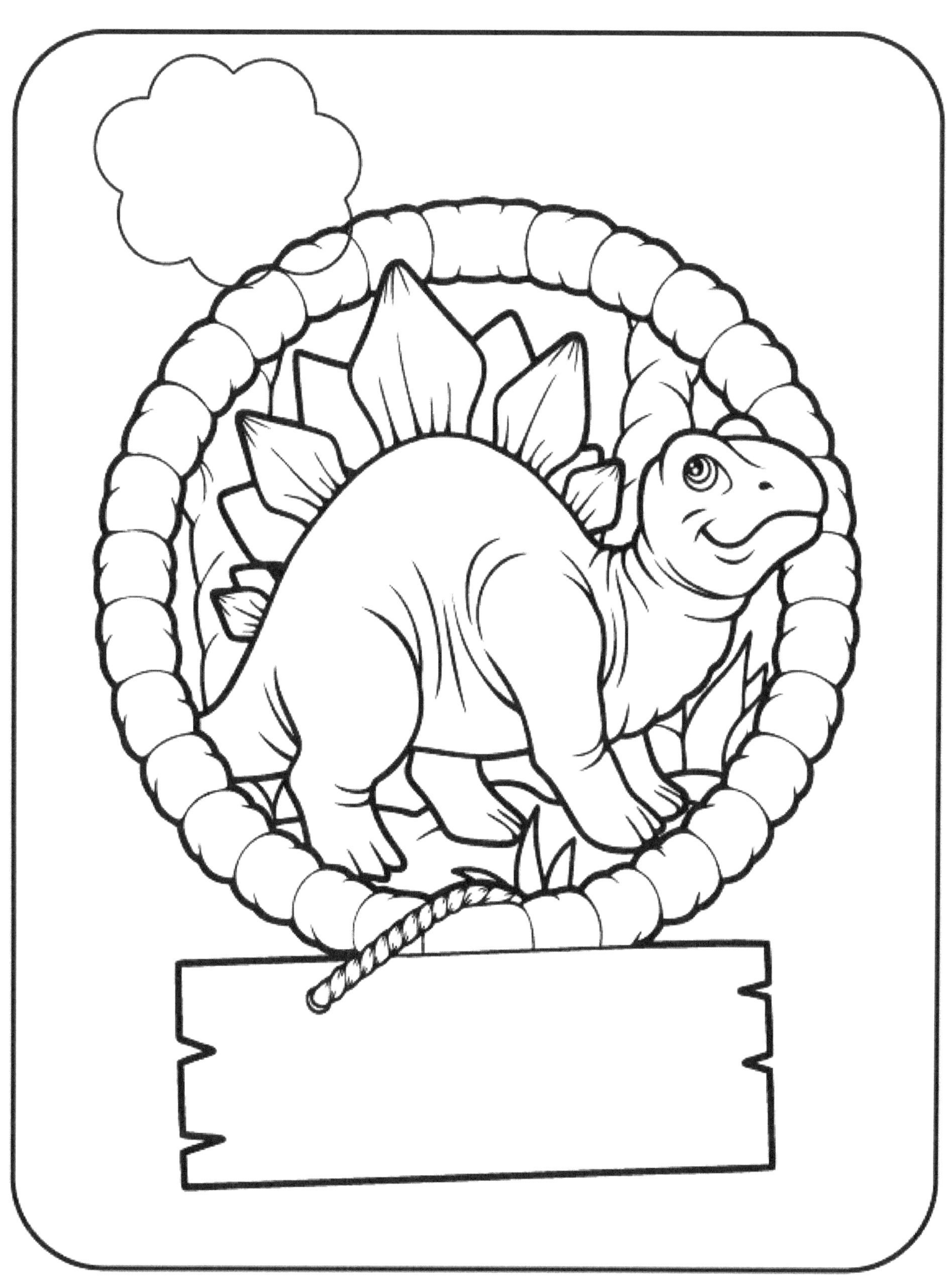

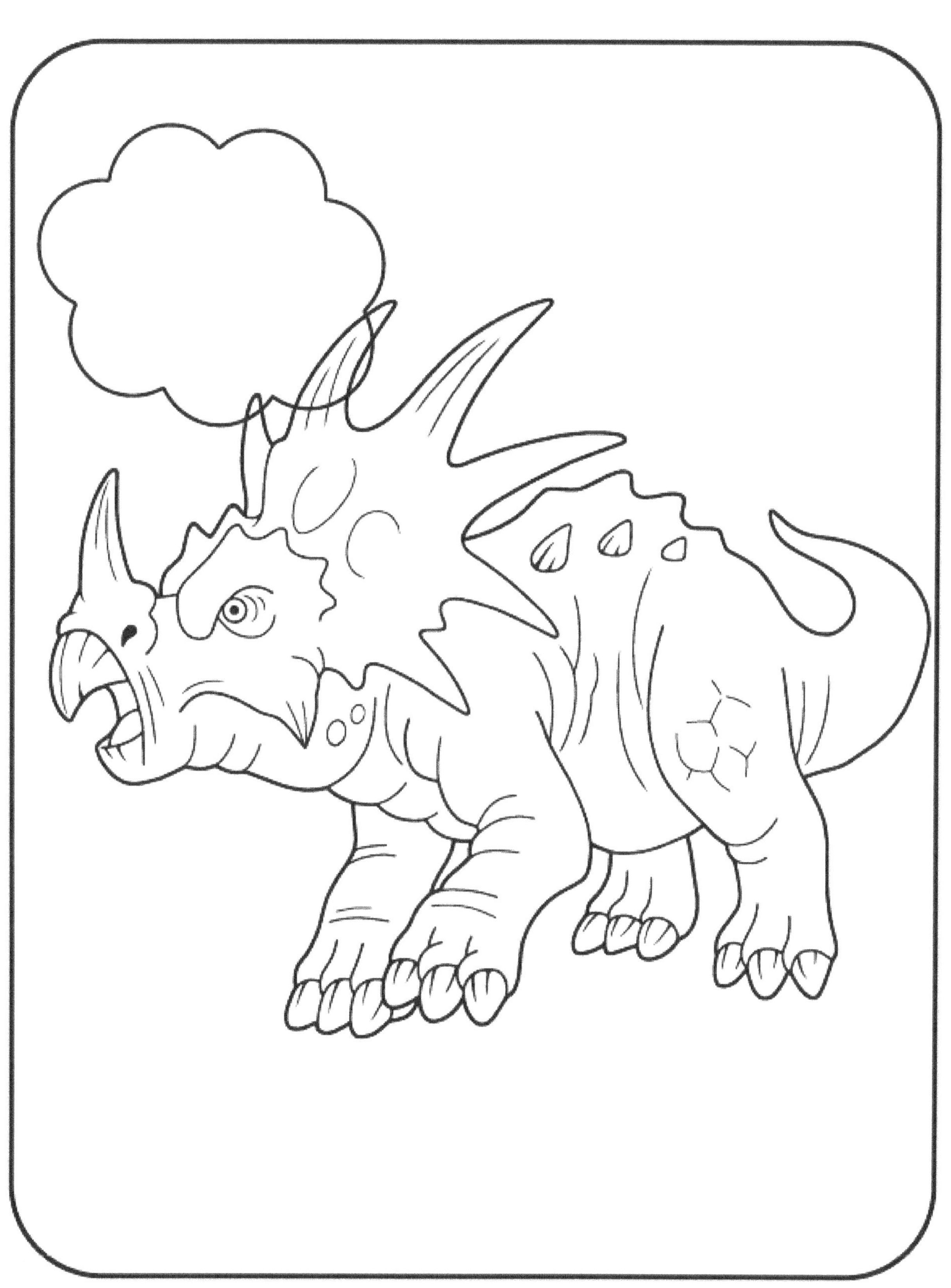

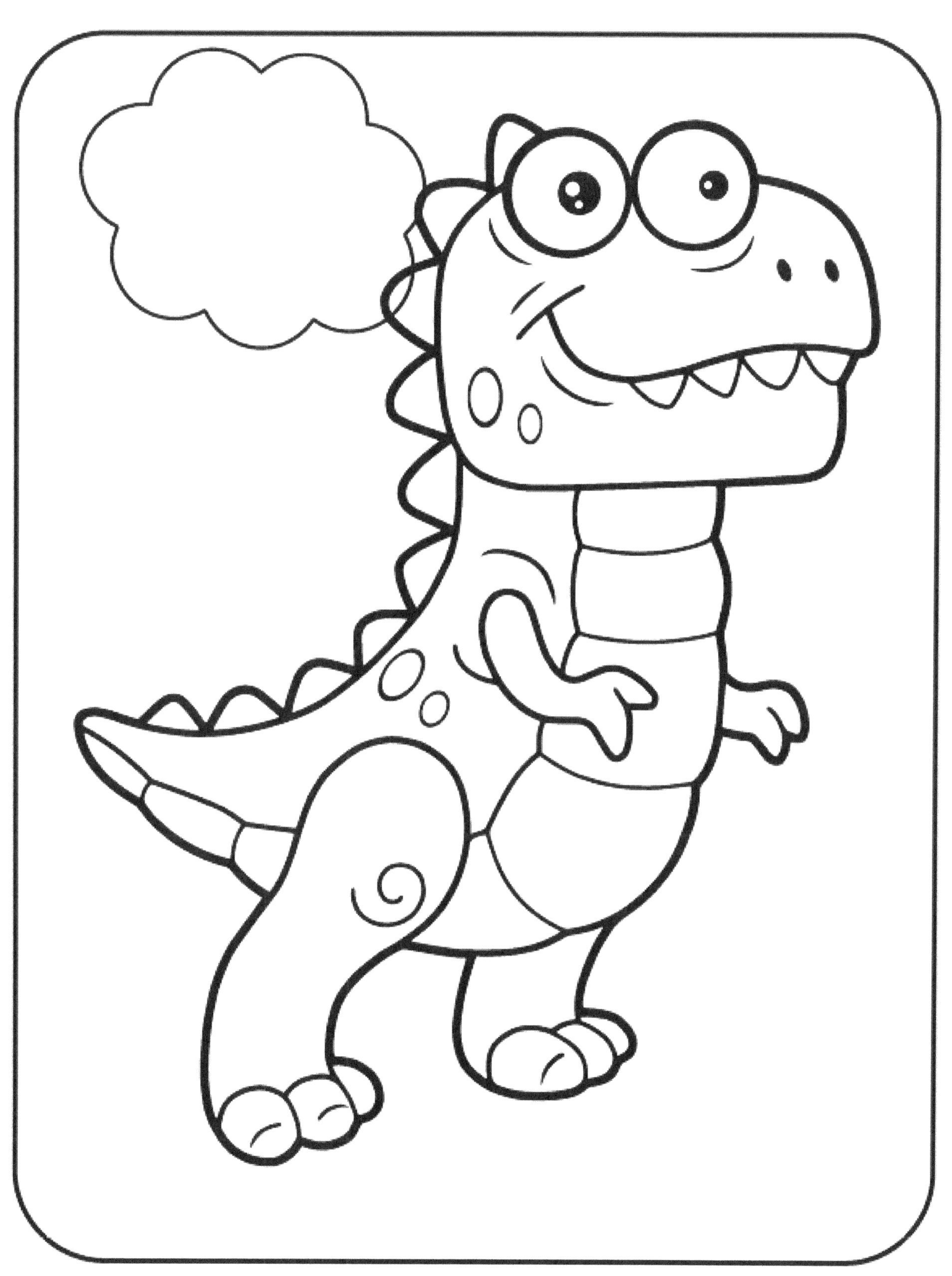

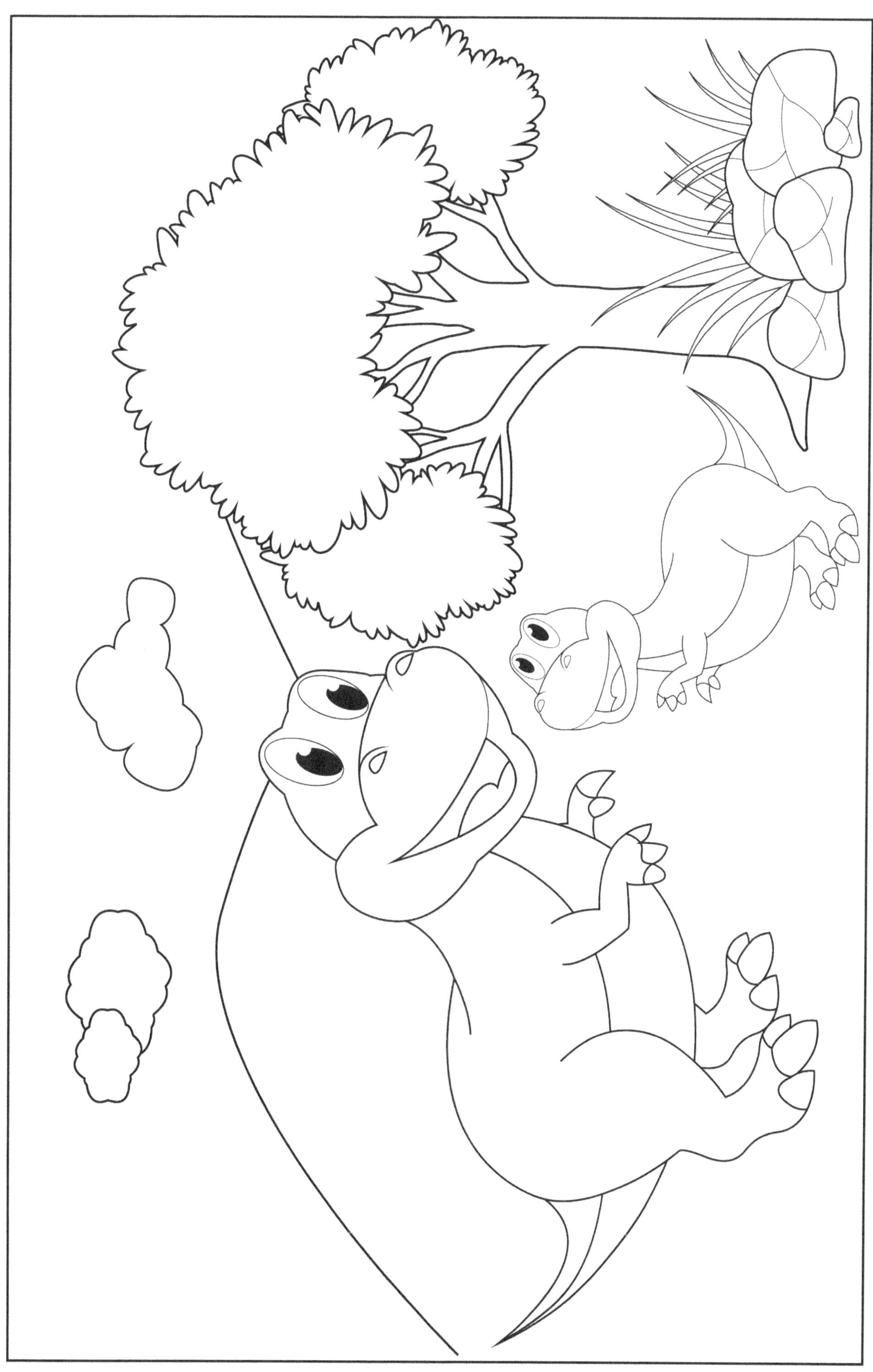

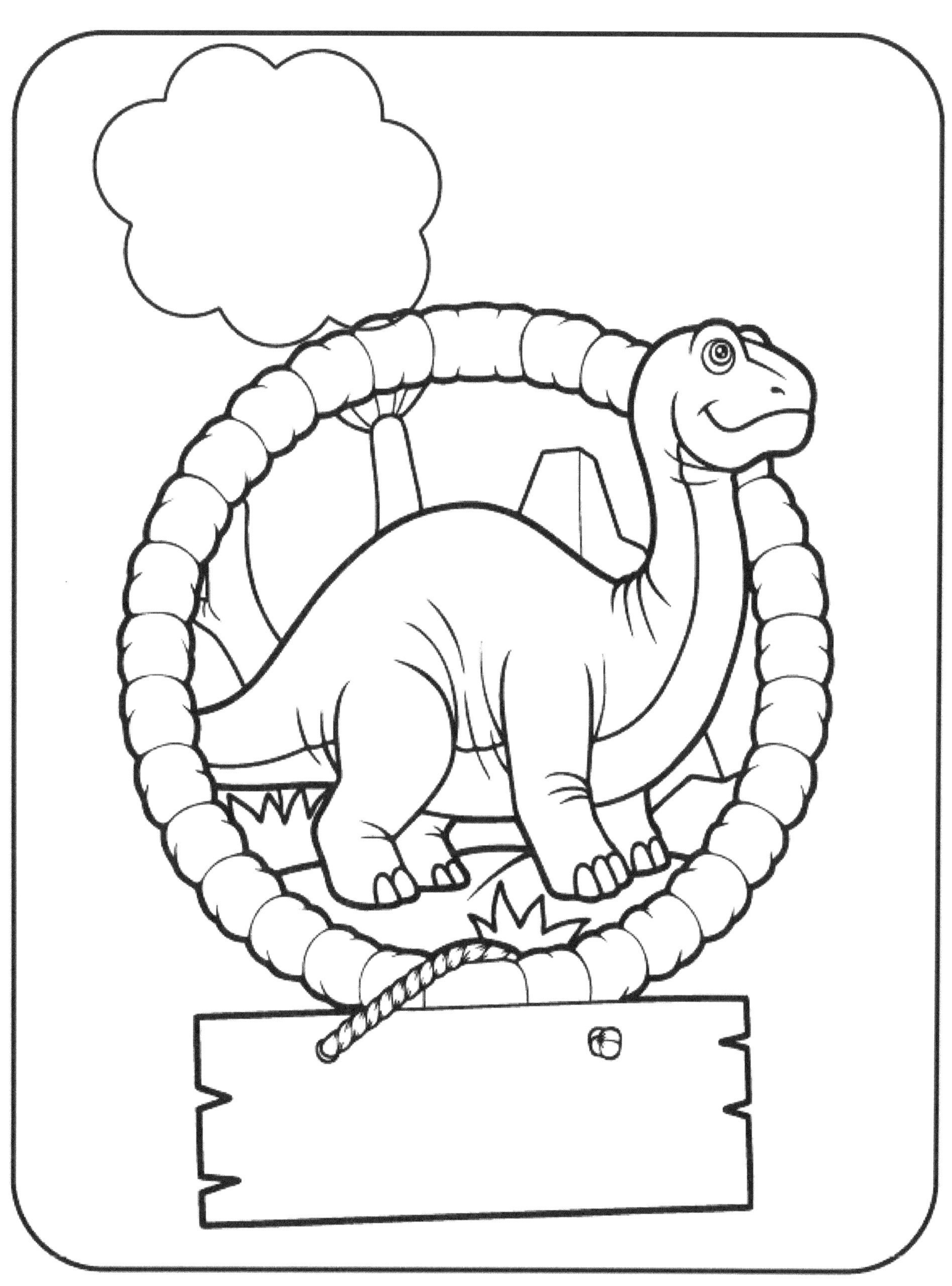

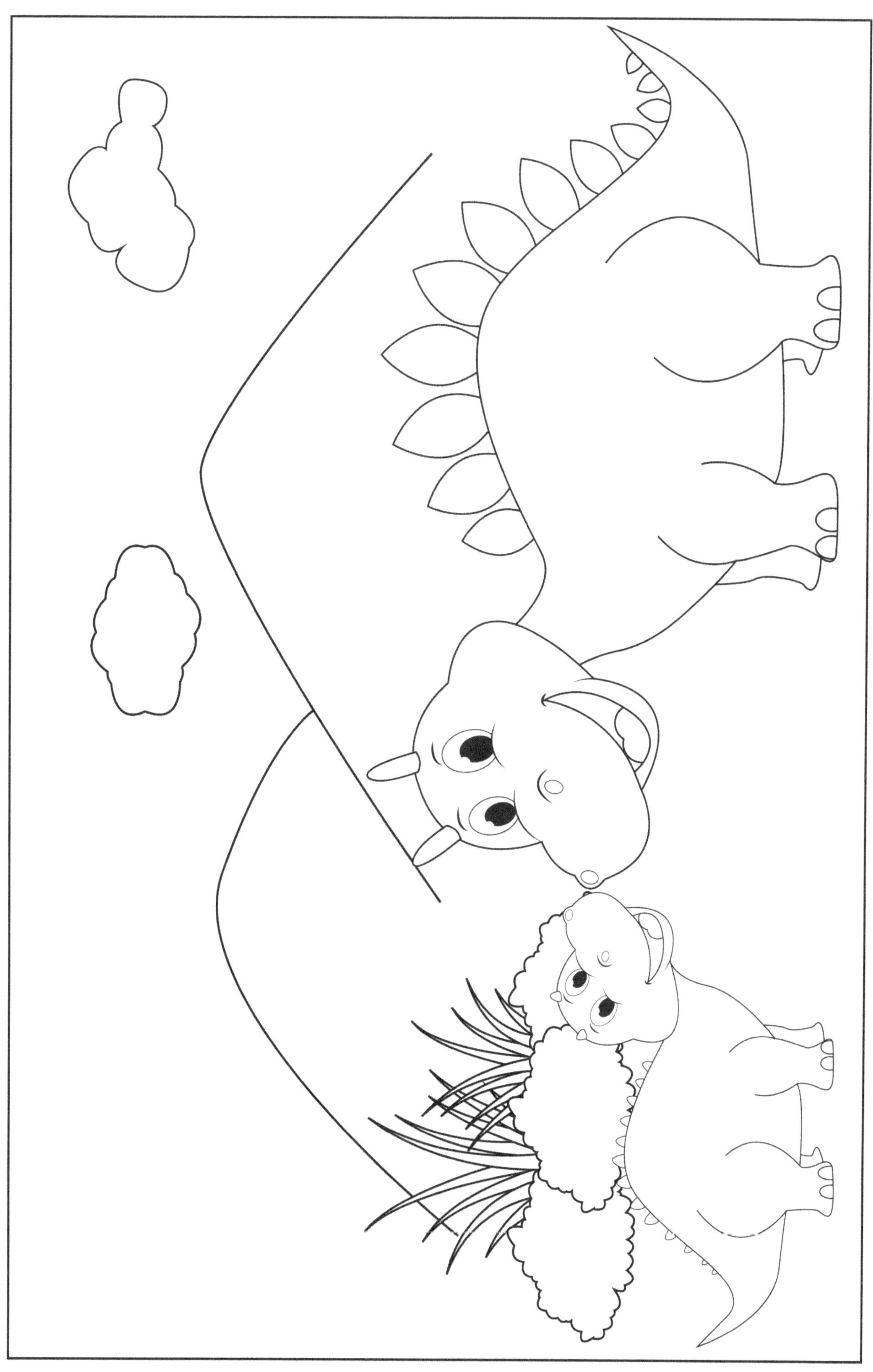

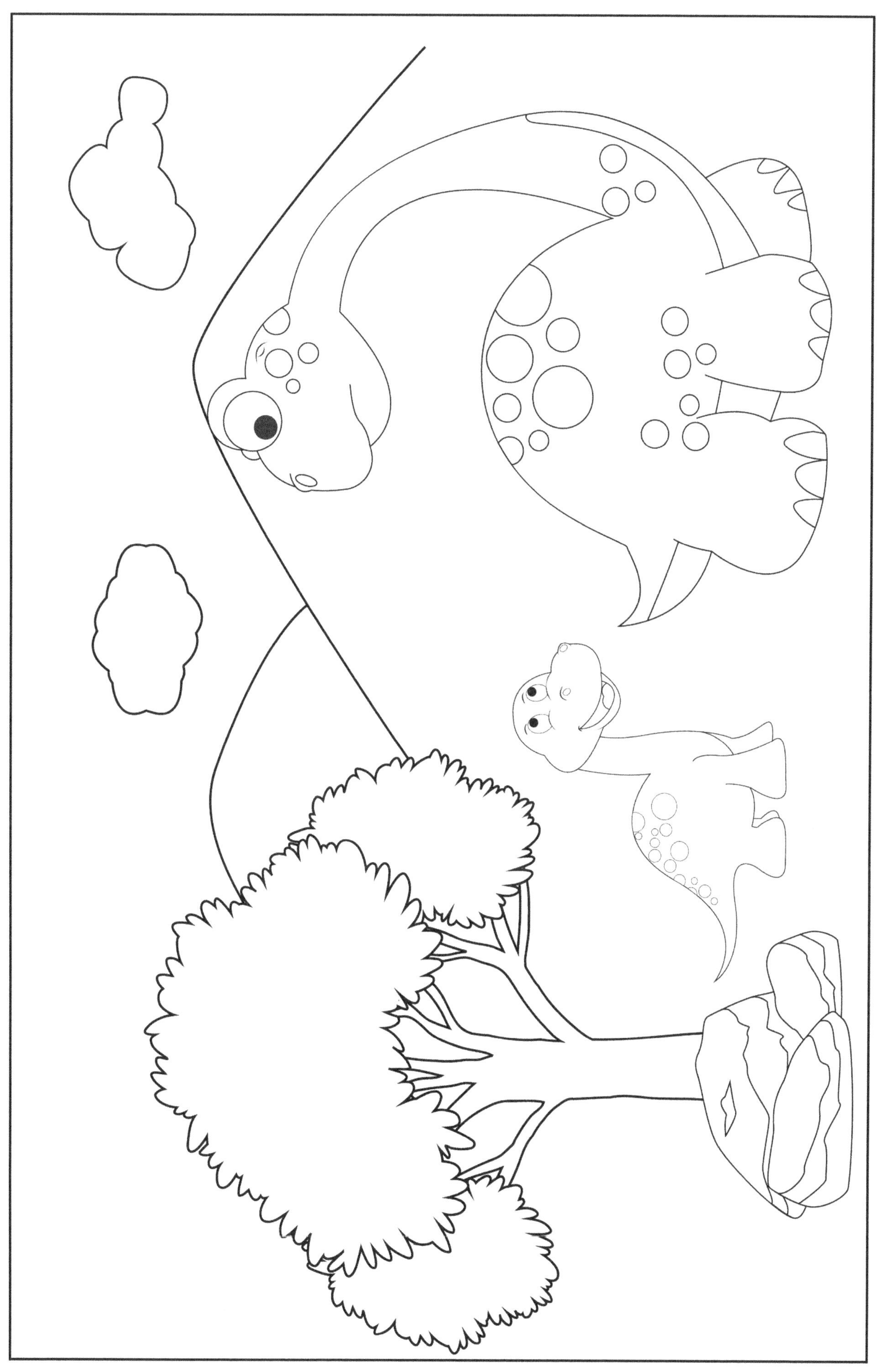

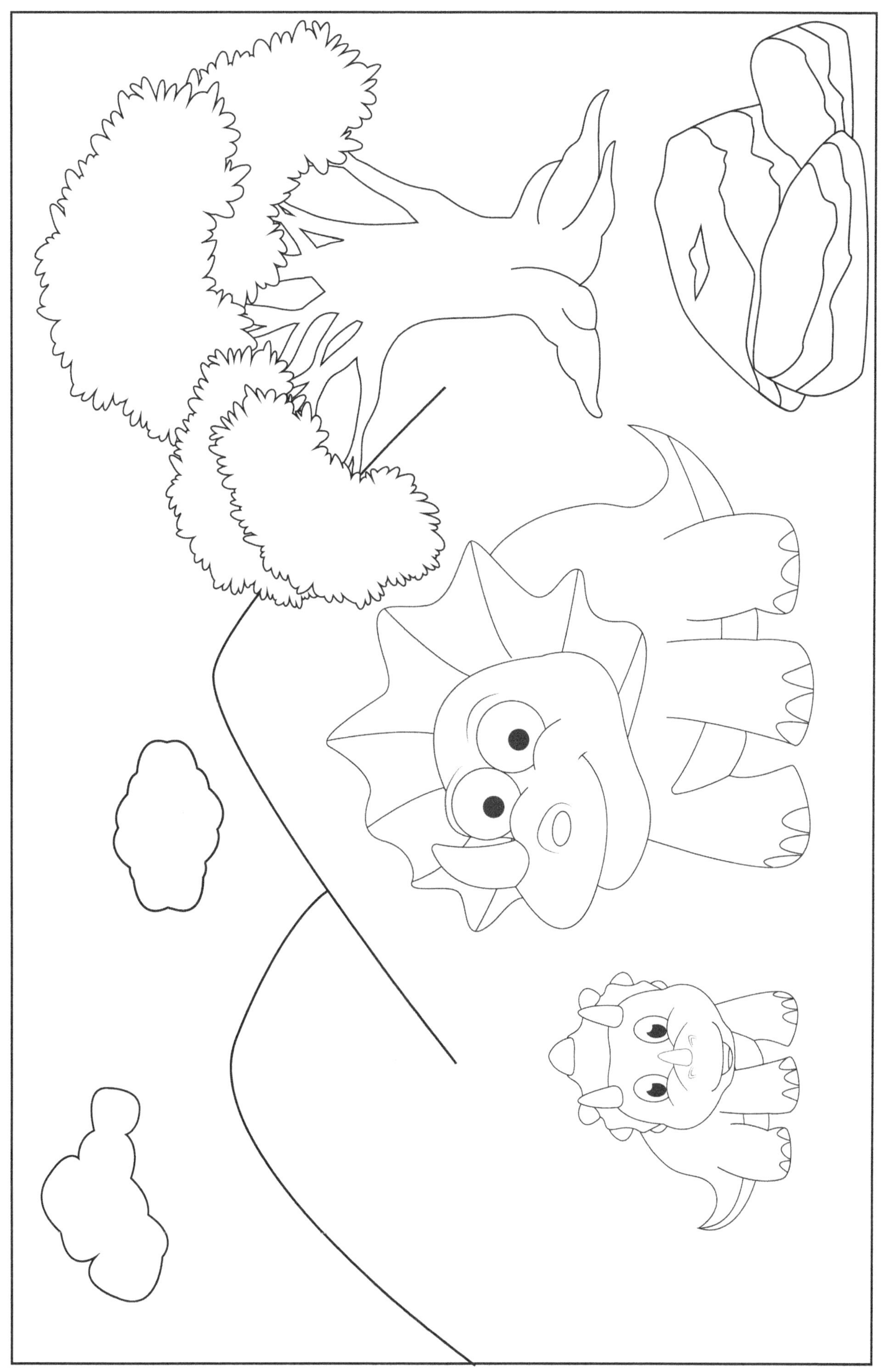

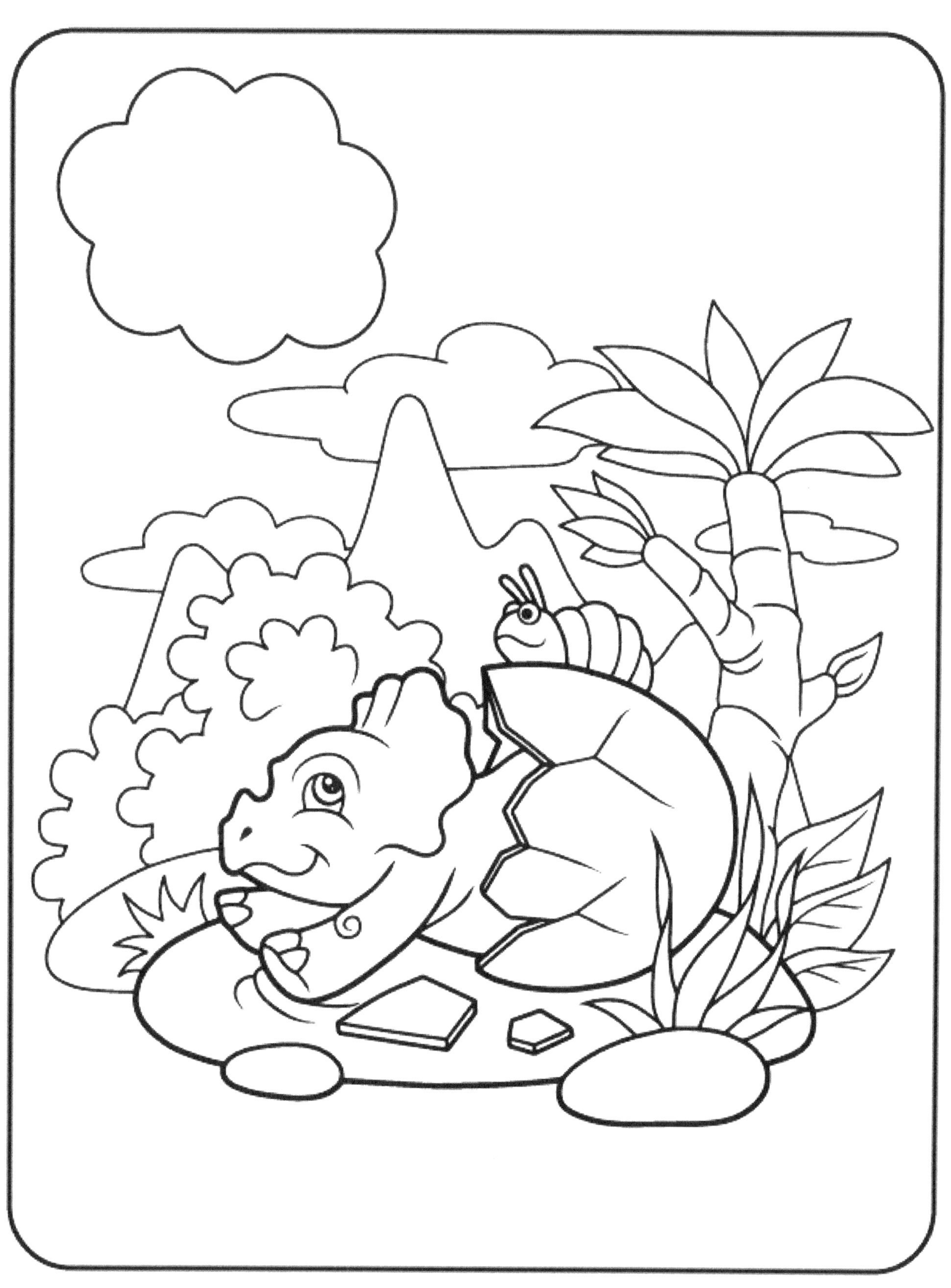